Also by Lucinda Berry Hill:

Hope from a Friend
Joy from a Friend
Coffee with Jesus

A Second Cup with Jesus

52 weeks of inspiration

Lucinda Berry Hill

Prayers written by Linda Turner Palmer

WESTBOW

P R E S S

A DIVISION OF THOMAS NELSON
& ZONDERVAN

Scripture taken from the Holy Bible, NEW INTERNATIONAL VERSION®. Copyright © 1973, 1978, 1984 by Biblica, Inc. All rights reserved worldwide. Used by permission. NEW INTERNATIONAL VERSION® and NIV® are registered trademarks of Biblica, Inc. Use of either trademark for the offering of goods or services requires the prior written consent of Biblica US, Inc.

WestBow Press books may be ordered through booksellers or by contacting:

WestBow Press
A Division of Thomas Nelson & Zondervan
1663 Liberty Drive
Bloomington, IN 47403
www.westbowpress.com
1 (866) 928-1240

ISBN: 978-1-4908-5963-7 (sc)
ISBN: 978-1-4908-5965-1 (hc)
ISBN: 978-1-4908-5964-4 (e)

Library of Congress Control Number: 2014920616

Printed in the United States of America.

WestBow Press rev. date: 11/19/2014

Contents

Introduction: First Thing's First ix

Week 1:   God's Plans 1

Week 2:   His Right Arm 3

Week 3:   Message from the Sun 5

Week 4:   Troubles? 7

Week 5:   The Baggage Carrier 9

Week 6:   Who Is The Holy Spirit? 11

Week 7:   Too Busy 13

Week 8:   The Donkey 17

Week 9:   Prayer by Prayer 19

Week 10:   Invisible Me 21

Week 11:   He Died for Me 25

Week 12:   He Sees Us Through 27

Week 13:   The Cross of Christ in Your Life 29

Week 14:   You're Still on Your Feet 31

Week 15:   Not Enough Soup 33

Week 16:   Sycamore Trees 35

Week 17:   Your Pain, Their Blessing 37

Week 18:   I'm God's Somebody 39

Week 19:   When You Just Want to Go to Sleep 43

Week 20:   Just to Praise Him 45

Week 21:   Pick Up a Shovel 49

Week 22:   Seek Him 51

Week 23:   Do-Overs 53

Week 24:   Use Your Gifts 55

Week 25:   God the Knitter 57
Week 26:   Live Like You're Loved 59
Week 27:   Under Her Apron.. 61
Week 28:   Freedom.. 63
Week 29:   Don't Be Finished 65
Week 30:   A Holy Friend.. 67
Week 31:   Praising God During Difficult Times................. 69
Week 32:   Choices 71
Week 33:   He's Already There 73
Week 34:   Through the Fog.. 75
Week 35:   I Can't Do a Day Without Jesus 77
Week 36:   I Am Said I Will 79
Week 37:   God's Family in Harmony.............................. 83
Week 38:   God's Shadows 87
Week 39:   He Made Me Tougher 89
Week 40:   Fall in Love... 91
Week 41:   Pray for Your Heart...................................... 93
Week 42:   Finding Home... 95
Week 43:   A Sip, A prayer, A Peace................................. 99
Week 44:   How to Sleep Through a Storm 101
Week 45:   A God of Always... 103
Week 46:   God's Feet.. 105
Week 47:   Pressed and Praising 107
Week 48:   Meet Him in Your Prayers 109
Week 49:   Finding Joy in the Journey 113
Week 50:   All the Time 115
Week 51:   This Thing Called Life 117
Week 52:   Stumble and Fall 119
Something Special: God Whispers in the Wind 121
Topical Index 123
Scripture Index 127
Christian Website Links 129

With our hands raised high and a song of praise on our lips, we dedicate this devotional book to our Lord and Savior, Jesus Christ. None of this would be possible without Him.

We thank our families for their encouragement and patience. Their love and endless prayer and support means more than they'll ever know.

For those who are familiar with our work and those who have yet to read our work, we pray that God will richly bless your life as you use this devotional book.

Lucinda Berry Hill   Linda Turner Palmer

First Thing's First

First you say, "Good morning."
Thank Him for your day.
First you give Him glory.
Then you start to pray.
First you read His word,
Manna for the soul.
First you give to God.
Then you fill your bowl.
First you trust in Jesus.
Confess to Him your sin.
First He'll fix your spirit.
Then He'll fix your pain.
First you give Him time
Your day will fall in place.
First you go to Jesus
Asking Him in faith.
First you give your heart
To the Lord above.
He will give you Heaven.
First He'll give you love.

Week One

God's Plans

I don't know what Your plan is
But I know that I will prosper.
I don't know when the time will be
But I know Your time is right.
I don't know when I'll need some help
But I know You'll be my aid.
I don't know where I'm going
But I know You'll be my light.
I don't know what the future holds
But I know You hold the future.
I don't know what Your answer is
But I know Your word is true.
I don't know where You'll send me
But I know I'll go in joy.
I don't know what Your plan is
But I know I'll trust in You.
For You, Lord, have plans to give me hope and a future.

Jeremiah 29:10-13
This is what the LORD says: "When seventy years are
completed for Babylon, I will come to you and fulfill my
gracious promise to bring you back to this place. For I

know the plans I have for you," declares the LORD, "plans to prosper you and not to harm you, plans to give you hope and a future. Then you will call upon me and come and pray to me, and I will listen to you. You will seek me and find me when you seek me with all your heart.

Dear God,
You have s specific plan for my life. There's a purpose that only I have and can fulfill. You didn't just put me on the planet to take up oxygen, but to do something wonderful with this life. Thank you! In Jesus' name, Amen.

Week Two

His Right Arm

When a child is tired,
He clings to the arm of his mother.
A blind man may be guided by the arm of a friend.
A weak and hurting woman could be held up
By the arm of her husband.
When I'm tired
I rest in God's arms.
When I can't see what's ahead, I clutch at His right hand.
When I'm hurting and struggling,
I cling to the right arm of my Savior.
When I'm happy and excited, I pull at His right arm,
"Did you see that Father? Did you see that?"
God's arm
And His love
Are steadfast and never-ending.
I cling to it each day as I walk and wait for His return.

Psalm 89:13–15
Your arm is endued with power, your hand is strong,
your right hand exalted. Righteousness and justice are the
foundation of your throne; love and faithfulness go before

3

you. Blessed are those who have learned to acclaim you,
who walk in the light of your presence, O LORD.

My Abba Daddy,
Thank You for letting me stand by Your right side and grab
on to Your mighty arm when I'm frightened, or rest there
when I'm so weary I can't take another step. Thank You for
encouraging me when no one else does. I know I really can't
do anything without You. My accomplishments are not mine,
but Yours. I praise You for all that You do through me.
In Jesus' Name I humbly pray, Amen.

Week Three

Message from the Sun

In the sky God placed the sun,
I think for us to see
That wherever we may go in life
His Son will always be.
The same God watches over us.
The same sun we see.
And like the sun up in the sky
God's Son leads you and me.
Sometimes it seems He's gone away,
It seems the clouds have won.
But in some time the clouds will leave
And there remains the Son.
Always there, bright and strong,
The sun it seems to say,
"God is always here for you.
His Son is here to stay."

Deuteronomy 31:6-8
Be strong and courageous. Do not be afraid or terrified
because of them, for the LORD your God goes before
you; he will never leave you nor forsake you." Then Moses
summoned Joshua and said to him in the presence of all

Israel, "Be strong and courageous, for your must go with this people into the land that the LORD swore to their forefathers to give them, and you must divide it among them as their inheritance. The LORD himself goes before you and will be with you; he will never leave you or forsake you. Do not be afraid; do not be discouraged."

Lord of Creation,
What a wonderful feeling to see the sun in the sky!
We take the rising and setting of the sun for granted.
Forgive our neglect of that daily miracle. May we not take your Son, Jesus, for granted in our lives either.
It's in His matchless Name we pray, Amen.

Week Four

Troubles?

What if
I gave them to Jesus?
What if
I left them with him?
Only good
Could come of my troubles.
Only good
Is given by Him.
Hurtful words,
Sickness, and tension
What if
I gave them to Him.
Disrespect,
Lies, and deception
What if
I left them with Him.
Stress at work,
Pain, and misfortune
Jesus can take them for me.
Loneliness,
Debt, and affliction
He can replace them with peace.
What if

I gave them to Jesus?
What if
I left them with Him?
Only good
Could come of my troubles.
Only good
Is given by Him.

Isaiah 26:3-8
You will keep in perfect peace him whose mind is steadfast, because he trusts in you. Trust in the LORD forever, for the LORD, the LORD, is the Rock eternal. He humbles those who dwell on high, he lays the lofty city low; he levels it to the ground and casts it down to the dust. Feet trample it down—the feet of the oppressed, the footsteps of the poor. The path of the righteous is level; O upright One, you make the way of the righteous smooth. Yes, LORD, walking in the way of your laws, we wait for you; your name and renown are the desire of our hearts.

Dear Lord,
I pray Your peace over every concern on my mind today. I place them at Your feet and leave them there. Now I back away, singing praises to You and knowing that in Your own time, in Your own unique and creative way, You will fix everything. I have faith in You and refuse to listen to anyone who would tell me that my faith is misplaced. I have proven You true. What You say, You will do!
In Jesus' Name, Amen.

Week Five

The Baggage Carrier

A women is loaded down
With bags of shame and guilt.
A beautiful man goes to her and says,
"Here, let Me take these for you."
An old man is burdened
With bags of sin and embarrassment.
The same beautiful man goes to him and says,
"Here, let Me take these for you."
All around the world, this man goes
Taking baggage from everyone in need.
But He never gets overloaded with baggage Himself.
Why?
Because He discards them and mentions them no more.
Let Jesus take your baggage.
Let Him take your hand.
Your baggage He'll forget.
Your hand, He'll never let go of.

Psalm 145:13-19
The LORD is faithful to all his promises and loving toward
all he has made. The LORD upholds all those who fall and
lifts up all who are bowed down. The eyes of all look to you,

and you give them their food at the proper time. You open
your hand and satisfy the desires of every living thing. The
LORD is righteous in all his ways and loving toward all he has
made. The LORD is near to all who call on him, to all who
call on him in truth. He fulfills the desires of those who fear
him, to all who call on him in truth. He fulfills the desires
of those who fear him; he hears their cry and saves them.

Dear God,
I can't hide anything from You. The baggage I carry through
life contains guilt, shame, and embarrassment. I thank
You that Jesus gently suggests that I let Him take those
bags and toss them into the forgetfulness sea! A weight is
then lifted from my soul and I am happy in my Christian
walk! Only then can I be an effective witness for You.
In Jesus' Name, Amen.

Week Six

Who Is The Holy Spirit?

He's the Spirit of God.
He lives everywhere.
Where're we go
He will be there.He's the all-knowing Spirit,
he Teacher of truth.
He lives inside me
And will live inside you.
He's powerful and holy.
He's a Helper to all.
He's someone, not something
And knows and sees all.
He's the Spirit of God,
The Spirit eternal.
He is ever present and
Will always be faithful.

John 14:15-17
"If you love me, you will obey what I command. And I will
ask the Father and he will give you another Counselor to
be with you forever the Spirit of truth. The world cannot
accept him, because it neither sees him nor knows him. But
you know him, for he lives with you and will be in you.

Precious Holy Spirit,
Please help me to examine my own life, my motives, my
moods, my sins,--next to the illuminating light of the
Word of God, The Holy Bible. Help my soul to always be
sensitive to Your desire for me to turn from my wicked
ways and seek God's way, which is always a better way.
In the matchless Name of Jesus I pray, Amen.

Week Seven

Too Busy

I'm too busy praying.
Too busy in hope,
I'm too busy waiting.
Too busy to mope.
I'm too busy asking.
Too busy in praise.
I'm too busy singing
To ever complain.
I'm too busy serving.
Too busy in prayer.
I'm too busy giving
To be in despair.
I'm too busy bowing.
Too busy on my knees.
Too busy being thankful
To ever lose my peace.

Psalm 145:18-21
The LORD is near to all who call on him, to all who
call on him in truth. He fulfills the desires of those who
fear him; he hears their cry, and saves them. The LORD
watches over all who love him, but all the wicked he will

destroy. My mouth will speak in praise of the LORD. Let every creature praise his holy name for ever and ever.

Father of Strength,
You've given me a certain number of days to live here. Please help me to be sensitive to the needs of others around me and grant that I may be the instrument You use to meet those needs. Keep me focused and enthusiastic with energy and purpose for the tasks ahead. I look forward to the next adventure You have planned for me.
In Jesus' Name, Amen.

The Donkey

If you throw water on a duck
It will run off his back.
It won't hinder his journey.
It won't silence his quack.
When the penguins get cold
They all work together.
They get in a huddle,
And the Son warms their feathers.
If you throw dirt on a donkey
He'll shake it and then
He'll climb up on top
And there he will stand.
We should be like the donkey,
The penguins, and more
Overcoming our burdens
With the help of our Lord.
He gives us the knowledge,
The wisdom, the strength
To live lives of victory
By way of His Name.

1 John 5:3-5
This is love for God: to obey his commands. And his
commands are not burdensome, for everyone born of God
overcomes the world. This is the victory that has overcome
the world, even our faith. Who is it that overcomes the
world? Only he who believes that Jesus is the Son of God.

Father God,
I don't know why some things have to happen in life,
but I know You use everything for Your purpose
and to strengthen me. Take these burdens from me
because it's Your desire that I live a victorious life in
You. Thank You for what You will do in my life!
In Jesus' Name, Amen.

Week Nine

Prayer by Prayer

Step by step.
Stair by stair.
Getting through each day
Prayer by prayer.
Bit by bit.
With great care.
I will get through this
Prayer by prayer.
It might happen tomorrow.
It might happen next week.
But I'm gonna make it
Down here on my knees.
It seems it's a struggle
Day in and day out.
I need to have faith
Without fear, without doubt.
Moment by moment.
With patience to spare.
Breath by breath.
Prayer by prayer.

Day by day
My words will declare,
"I'm going to make it!
Prayer by prayer!"

1 Chronicles 16:8-13.
Give thanks to the LORD, call on his name; make known
among the nations what he has done. Sing to him, sing
praise to him; tell of all his wonderful acts. Glory in his
holy name, let the hearts of those who seek the LORD
rejoice. Look to the LORD and his strength; see his face
always. Remember the wonders he has done, his miracles,
and the judgments he pronounced, O descendants of
Israel his servant, O sons of Jacob, his chosen ones.

Dear Lord,
Prayer is a conversation that happens between the two of us.
Help me do just as much listening as talking, and help me have
the patience to wait for Your perfect timing for answers.
In Jesus' Name, Amen.

Week Ten

Invisible Me

When I'm feeling unappreciated,
When I'm feeling overworked,
When I'm feeling disregarded,
When I'm feeling overlooked,
Lord, help me to find comfort
In giving it to You.
May you receive the glory
For all that I must do.
Remind me of the lesson
That I am here to serve;
To be Your hands of giving
According to Your word.
Nothing goes unnoticed.
Nothing gets past You.
Others may not see me
But I'm significant to You.
And help me see Your goodness
In each and every day
And let me never
Ignore You,
Your provisions, or Your grace.

Hebrews 6:10-12

God is not unjust; he will not forget your work and the love
that you have shown him as you have helped his people and
continue to help them. We want each of you to show this same
diligence to the very end, in order to make your hope sure.
We do not want you to become lazy, but to imitate those who
through faith and patience inherit what has been promised.

Lord of Love,
I've felt so isolated, alone, and ignored lately. Help me to
remember that even if people don't notice or recognize
me, You do. You love me and think I'm special.
Thank You. In Jesus' Name, Amen.

Week Eleven

He Died for Me

He died for me.
Christ died for me.
He took my sin upon His back
He set me free
When He died for me.
I'm so thankful.
So very thankful.
The punishment I so deserve
I could not handle
So glad He died for me.
What a Savior.
My Holy Savior.
A beautiful man of flesh.
He showed me favor
When He died for me.
I praise my Hero.
My soul's Defender.
When He returns
His gates I'll enter
Because He died for me.

Thank You Jesus
King of Kings.
You took my soul
And washed it clean
When You died for me.

1 John 2:1-2
My dear children, I write this to you so that you will not
sin. But if anybody does sin, we have one who speaks to
the Father in our defense—Jesus Christ, the Righteous
One. He is the atoning sacrifice for our sins, and not
only for ours but also for the sins of the whole world.

Heavenly Father,
Thank You so much for sending Your only Son into this
wicked world to willingly give His life for my sins. What
a price He paid and I'm so unworthy, but so very grateful.
I praise You for Your plan of salvation for all mankind.
In Jesus' Name, Amen.

Week Twelve

He Sees Us Through

Sometimes the tunnel seems so dark
And sometimes it seems so long.
But I know you'll make it to the end
If you just keep on moving on.
Knowing God is for you,
Believing in His might,
Will help you make it through each day
And through each darkened night.
There's light at the end of the tunnel.
I know this to be true.
Jesus, He's the light that shines
And He will lead you through.

Psalm 71:19-22

Your righteousness reaches to the skies, O God, you who have
done great things. Who, O God, is like you? Though you have
made me see troubles, many and bitter, you will restore my life
again; from the depths of the earth you will again bring me
up. You will increase my honor and comfort me once again. I
will praise you with the harp for your faithfulness, O my God;
I will sing praise to you with the lyre, O Holy One of Israel.

Lord of Light,
I'm afraid to keep walking because the path looks so dark, but
You will show me the right road to take and in hindsight I
will once again marvel at how You led me back into the light.
I praise You for Your faithfulness when I show so little faith.
In Jesus' Name, Amen.

Week Thirteen

The Cross of Christ in Your Life

Can they see it?
Can they see the cross of Christ?
Can they see the cross of Christ in your life?
I know sometimes we slip.
We're not always on the mark.
Sometimes we do get angry,
Frustrated, and sharp.
But we must always carry Jesus
In our hearts and in our hands.
Doing things that pleases Him,
The One for which we stand.
Don't let the clouds control you
Or take away your light.
Make sure the cross of Jesus
Is seen throughout your life.
So others who are struggling
Feeling burdened, hurt, or lost
Will see their way to freedom,
Through your life, Christ on the cross.

Ephesians 4:1-3
As a prisoner for the Lord, then, I urge you to live
a life worthy of the calling you have received. Be
completely humble and gentle; be patient, bearing
with one another in love. Make every effort to keep
the unity of the Spirit through the bond of peace.

Father,
I think I know how Peter felt right after the rooster crowed.
I blew it major big time! Please Lord, please forgive me
and restore unto me the joy of my salvation. The cross that
Jesus died on is the most important thing to me. I don't
know how I could have messed up so badly, except I am
so human sometimes. Please give me another opportunity
to let Your light shine where I failed to do so today.
Thank You, Lord. In Jesus' Name, Amen.

Week Fourteen

You're Still on Your Feet

I'm down on my knees God
And You're still on Your feet.
I'm lost and I'm tired.
I'm growing so weak.
But You have a plan God,
Please take control.
I'm bruised and I'm broken
But You are still whole.
I'm down on my knees God.
I'm tired, I'm stretched.
I'm worn out. I'm busted.
I'm gasping for breath.
I've hit the hard bottom.
The next step I can't see.
But the thing that I'm clinging to,
Is You're still on Your feet!
I can't seem to hang on, Lord.
I'm losing my grip.
But You can hold everything
Your hands they won't slip.

Your love keeps me going.
Your ways give me peace.
I'm down on my knees, God
And You,
You're still on your feet!

Psalm 121

I lift up my eyes to the hills—where does my help come from?
My help comes from the LORD, the Maker of heaven and
earth. He will not let your foot slip—he who watches over you
will not slumber; indeed, he who watches over Israel will never
slumber or sleep. The LORD watches over you—the LORD
is your shade at your right hand; the sun will not harm you by
day, nor the moon at night. The LORD will keep you from
all harm—he will watch over your life; the LORD will watch
over your coming and going both now and forevermore.

God Who Never Slumbers,
Thank You for sending angels to surround me day and night.
I can sleep with complete peace of mind because You are
awake and watching over me. I don't have to be frightened
of the dark because You are the light of the world. I
can be tired because You never are. My weakness is acceptable
because I walk in Your strength. Thank You Abba Father.
In Jesus' Name, Amen.

Week Fifteen

Not Enough Soup

There's not enough bowls of soup.
There's not enough songs to sing.
You need to have God's glorious grace
To ever get close to the King.
There's not enough cups of water.
There's not enough kindness to show.
You need to have the grace of God
To get yourself near the throne.
There's not enough books for reading.
There's not enough checks or cash.
You need to have the grace of God
And you only need to ask.
There's always enough grace for saving.
There's always enough love from God.
His grace outweighs all your deeds.
And His Grace, it is enough.

Ephesians 2:8-10
For it is by grace you have been saved, through faith—
and this is not from yourselves, it is the gift of God—
not by works, so that no one can boast. For we are

God's workmanship, created in Christ Jesus to do good
works, which God prepared in advance for us to do.

Dear Lord of Limitless Mercy and Grace,
There is a limit to our resources, our strength and our
feeble efforts to please You. The good news is, there
is no limit to what You offer us in return! We have a
limitless supply of You! Your love, Your mercy, and
Your wonderful, matchless grace! We need only ask.
Thank you, LORD! In Jesus' Name, Amen.

Week Sixteen

Sycamore Trees

I want to be a Sycamore tree;
I want to lift another up.
I want to be a help to others
So they can see God's love.
Do you want to be a Sycamore tree,
Pointing your branches to the sky,
Leading the way to Glory
To the Glory of God on high?
We should all be Sycamore trees,
Using our leaves for shade
To shield and to protect God's children
'Till He calls us home by name.
Let us be like Sycamore trees.
Like the one in Jericho,
With our roots deeply planted
And God's seeds rich to sow.

Luke 19:1-6

Jesus entered Jericho and was passing through. A man
was there by the name of Zacchaeus; he was a chief tax
collector and was wealthy. He wanted to see who Jesus
was, but being a short man he could not, because of the

crowd. So he ran ahead and climbed a sycamore-fig tree
to see him, since Jesus was coming that way. When Jesus
reached the spot, he looked up and said to him, "Zacchaeus,
come down immediately. I must stay at your house today."
So he came down at once and welcomed him gladly.

Lord of Trees,
If I ever wished to be anything other than a human being,
it would be a Sycamore tree with the purpose that one
had for Zacchaeus. Because of it, he was able to see Jesus
above the crowd. I want to help people see Jesus above
the crowd too. I ask for Your help in doing that. Thank
You for giving my life purpose. In Jesus' Name, Amen.

Week Seventeen

Your Pain, Their Blessing

If you've ever stumbled,
Fallen flat on your face,
Got back up and
Received God's grace,
If you've ever fallen,
Been tested and tried,
Let it be a lesson
A word to the wise.
If you've ever wondered
Why God allows pain,
Your story's a warning
To teach and to train.
Just like the Israelites
From Egypt to Cannon,
Your story's a lesson
To stay far from sin.
Share your misfortune,
The lessons, the cost.
Let God make it a blessing
To those who're lost.

1 Corinthians 10:1-6
For I do not want you to be ignorant of the fact, brothers,
that our forefathers were all under the cloud and that they all
passed through the sea. They were all baptized into Moses
in the cloud and in the sea. They all ate the same spiritual
food and drank the same spiritual drink; for they drank
from the same spiritual rock that accompanied them, and
that rock was Christ. Nevertheless, God was not pleased
with most of them; their bodies were scattered over the
desert. Now these things occurred as examples to keep
us from setting our hearts on evil things as they did.

Father,
I know my life has not been perfect, but I thank You
for helping me along. I thank You that everything
works to the good and can be used to help others
learn about You and Your beautiful grace.
In Jesus' Name, Amen.

Week Eighteen

I'm God's Somebody

I was told I was a nobody,
A loser, and a waste.
That I'd always be incompetent,
Easily replaced.
I'd never be a somebody,
Never have success;
This is what was told to me,
I'd always be a mess.
I'd never have a hand to hold,
Never have a love.
I'd never 'mount to anything,
Just a failure, not enough.
I was told I was a nobody,
A nothing, a nonentity.
But hey!
God doesn't make nobodies.
I'm a child of the King!
He says I am a somebody,
A survivor, I'm a voice.
I always was a somebody
And to God I am a choice.

Psalm 138:4-8

May all the kings of the earth praise you, O LORD, when they hear the words of your mouth. May they sing of the ways of the LORD, for the glory of the LORD is great. Though the LORD is on high, he looks upon the lowly, but the proud he knows from afar. Though I walk in the midst of trouble, you preserve my life; you stretch out your hand against the anger of my foes, with your right hand you save me. The LORD will fulfill (his purpose) for me; your love, O LORD, endures forever—do not abandon the works of your hands.

God of Love,

You love me perfectly. The enemy of my soul is the one who wants to see me crash and burn. He is the one who puts ugly thoughts in my brain about myself. Help me to stop those ugly thoughts in their tracks and begin to praise You. Help me to remember that You made me and You love me like no one else ever will. Thank You for Your precious Holy Spirit. May I dance with Your joy in my heart!
In Jesus' Name, Amen.

Week Nineteen

When You Just Want to Go to Sleep

Curl up in the blanket of God's goodness.
Rest your head upon His pillow of grace.
Wrap your arms around the comfort of His presence.
Find peace in His mattress of strength.
Find warmth in His arms that will hold you.
Let God's mercy be your soft place to land.
Rest your mind on His cushion of power.
Be cradled in the palm of His hand.
Close your door, shut your eyes, stop your thinking.
Let God's voice be all that you hear.
Be still in the love that enfolds you.
For the joy in the morning is near.

Psalm 4:5-8

Offer right sacrifices and trust in the LORD. Many are
asking, "Who can show us any good?" Let the light
of your face shine upon us, O LORD. You have filled
my heart with greater joy then when their grain and
new wine abound. I will lie down and sleep in peace,
for you alone, O LORD, make me dwell in safety.

Precious Lord,
Sometimes at night my mind won't shut off. Please
help me to give all of those racing thoughts to You
for safe keeping. They will keep until tomorrow.
Thank You, Father God. In Jesus' Name, Amen.

Just to Praise Him

The Lord is my Shepherd
I shall not want
Anything
But to praise Him.
He restores my soul.
He gives me strength
To follow His lead
And to praise Him.
He'll give all that I need
Until there'll be
Not a thing left
But to praise Him.
I don't live in fear.
The Lord, He is here,
Every step of the way
So I praise Him.
He's anointed my head.
My cup overflows
With words and with song
To praise Him.

His goodness and mercy
Will follow me long.
I will dwell in His house.
And I'll praise Him.
The Lord is my Shepherd
I shall not want
Anything
But to praise Him.

Psalm 138:1-4
I will praise you, O LORD, with all my heart; before the
"gods" I will sing your praise. I will bow down toward your
holy temple and will praise your name for your love and your
faithfulness, for you have exalted above all things your name
and your word. When I called, you answered me; you made
me bold and stouthearted. May all the kings of the earth praise
you, O LORD, when they hear the words of your mouth.

Dear Kind and Loving Heavenly Father,
Because You are everything to me, how can I do
anything but praise You? I praise You with my words,
actions, and with my everyday life! Thank You for saving
my soul and keeping me safe throughout my life.
In Jesus' Name, Amen.

Week Twenty One

Pick Up a Shovel

God can move mountains
But sometimes He may
Hand you a shovel
To work through your faith.
He'll give you a shovel,
A pick, and an ax.
He'll give you the strength,
The courage to act.
You cannot sit idol
And expect things to change.
If you want mountains to move
You have to work with your faith.
God can move mountains
At the sound of His voice.
But sometimes God's quiet
Till you make a choice.
Do you have a mountain
You want out of the way?
It takes shovels of patience,
Of prayers, and of praise.

God can move mountains
We know this is true.
Pick up a shovel
And pray 'till it's moved.

2 Thessalonians 1:11-12
With this in mind, we constantly pray for you, that our
God may count you worthy of his calling, and that by his
power he may fulfill every good purpose of yours and every
act prompted by your faith. We pray this so that the name
of our Lord Jesus may be glorified in you, and you in him,
according to the grace of our God and the Lord Jesus Christ.

Heavenly Guide,
I thank you for giving me all I need to live my life. You
know all too well the mountain I now have setting before
me. I refuse to worry about it because You've let me know
it won't change anything. Please give me more faith to
trust Your timing and Your perfect way of resolving this
issue. I don't have to know how You will do it, but I sure
need to have the faith and confidence that You will do it.
Thank You in advance for what You will do in my life.
In Jesus' Name, Amen.

Week Twenty Two

Seek Him

Seek Him when you're working,
When decisions you need to make.
Seek Him when you're hurting,
When a rest you need to take.
Seek Him when you're wondering,
He will answer you.
Seek Him when you're nervous,
He will give you courage too.
Seek Him when you're feeling weak,
He will make you strong.
Seek Him when you're playing,
He will bring to you a song.
Seek Him when you're loving,
He will give you more to love.
Seek the Lord and His goodness,
Seek Him, up above.

Psalm 105:1-5
Give thanks to the LORD, call on his name; make known
among the nations what he has done. Sing to him, sing
praise to him; tell of all his wonderful acts. Glory in his
holy name; let the hearts of those who seek the LORD

rejoice. Look to the LORD and his strength; seek his face always. Remember the wonders he has done, his miracles, and the judgments he pronounced, O descendants of Abraham his servant, O sons of Jacob, his chosen ones.

Father,

You whispered a phrase to me when I was very young, scared, and sitting at a big grand piano. You said, "Pray, then play." There are moments You speak to me that I will not forget and that's one of them. You've always been my Lord, but I thank you for being the One to bring peace to my soul when I need it most. Thank you for being there when I seek you. In Jesus' Name, Amen.

Week Twenty Three

Do-Overs

So many times we make mistakes
And we cannot turn back time
But God allows a second chance,
A do-over every time.
He'll pick us up when we fall.
He'll wipe away our tears.
He'll send us on to try again
As He stands beside and cheers.
Sometimes we may just stumble,
Make a blunder when we choose.
But God allows us second chances
And He will help us through.
So don't give up when you trip.
Don't stay in shame and sorrow.
God allows us do-overs
So be thankful for tomorrow.

Psalm 103:8-14
The LORD is compassionate and gracious, slow to anger,
abounding in love. He will not always accuse, nor will
he harbor his anger forever, he does not treat us as our
sins deserve or repay us according to our iniquities. For

as high as the heavens are above the earth, so great is his
love for those who fear him; as far as the east is from the
west, so far has he removed our transgressions from us.
As a father has compassion on his children, so the LORD
has compassion on those who fear him; for he knows
how we are formed, he remembers that we are dust.

Father,
I'm reminded by the story of Jonah that there are consequences
when I disobey Your command. I'm so thankful for the
second chances You give us when we choose to be stubborn.
You get our attention and set us back on the right path
because You love us so much. Thank You for loving us.
In Jesus' Name, Amen.

Week Twenty Four

Use Your Gifts

Today's the day to write for Jesus.
Use each day to share His word.
Those around you are the reason
Your gift from God must be heard.
Keep God's word close to your side.
He'll lead you by His word of words.
He'll show you things through your eyes;
Through what you see in His great world.
He wants to share with you, for others.
For you to share with them His love.
Be a light unto your brothers.
Live the words that you write of.
Fill the shelves with things you've written;
Stories, blogs, and notes to self.
Once you start there is no quittin'
God has written all Himself.
No matter what the gift you have is,
Use it, you will have rewards.
Music, writing, teaching kids;
Use it fully to bless the Lord.

1 Corinthians 12:4-11
There are different kinds of gifts, but the same Spirit. There are different kinds of service, but the same Lord. There are different kinds of working, but the same God works all of them in all men. Now to each one the manifestation of the Spirit is given for the common good. To one there is given through the Spirit the message of wisdom, to another the message of knowledge by means of the same Spirit, to another faith by the same Spirit, to another gifts of healing by that one Spirit, to another miraculous powers, to another prophecy, to another distinguishing between spirits, to another speaking in different kinds of tongues, and to still another the interpretation of tongues. All these are the work of one and the same Spirit, and he gives them to each one, just as he determines.

Lord of All Good Gifts,
May I do my very best because I want my accomplishments to shine for Your glory and honor today. I thank you for the gifts and the talents you have entrusted me with.
In Jesus' Name, Amen.

Week Twenty Five

God the Knitter

The Bible says that
God knit you together in your mother's womb.
Like the love and care of a knitter
Who carefully chooses her yarn and needles,
God carefully chose your eye color, the shape of your lips
And the size of your smile.
He made you able to serve Him, praise Him
And hold Him in the heart that He gave you.
Like the knitter, who puts love in every stitch that she makes,
God put His love in making you.
He had a plan.
He tenderly wove you together,
Making you one of a kind.
You are fearfully and wonderfully made.
To complete her project,
The knitter continues to
Slip the needle through,
Yarn over, and pull through.
God continues to watch over you and pull you through
Each and every day.
He created you, He loves you,
And He'll continue the good work He started in you.

Psalm 139:13–18
For you created my inmost being; you knit me together
in my mother's womb. I praise you because I'm fearfully
and wonderfully made; your works are wonderful, I know
that full well. My frame was not hidden from you when I
was made in the secret place. When I was woven together
in the depths of the earth, your eyes saw my unformed
body. All the days ordained for me were written in your
book before one of them came to be. How precious to
me are your thoughts, O God! How vast is the sum of
them! Were I to count them, they would outnumber the
grains of sand. When I awake, I am still with you.

God of Creation,
Thank You for making each one of us unique. Yet we
are similar enough that we can relate to one another.
You make no mistakes. May we never think You do by
making anyone feel inferior, including ourselves.
In Jesus' Name, Amen.

Week Twenty Six

Live Like You're Loved

God knows you're not perfect.
He knows that you'll fall.
But God still loves you
In spite of it all.
God helps those in need.
Does not matter who.
He's not 'bout Himself
But for me and for you.
He's slow to get angry
And quick to forgive.
And it is His will
For us to forgive.
God doesn't tell lies.
He speaks only the truth.
He believes in us all
And protects me and you.
God cherishes us
With an unending love.
He trains by example
So live like you're loved.

1 John 3:18 and 23-24
Dear children, let us not love in words or
tongue but with actions and in truth.
And this is his command: to believe in the name of
his Son, Jesus Christ, and to love one another as he
commanded us. Those who obey his commands live
in him, and he in them. And this is how we know that
he lives in us: We know it by the Spirit he gave us.

Father of Perfect Love,
There are no words to sufficiently express my thanks to You for
the love You bestow on me every day! You never give up on
me and I'm so grateful for Your love and forgiveness in my life.
May I give that same love to others. In Jesus' Name, Amen.

Under Her Apron

Under her apron
A woman, she prays.
Where no one can call her
Where no one can say, "Will you please do this...
Will you do that...
I can't find my keys...
I lost my new hat."
When she needs to be quiet
To hear the Lord's voice,
She goes under her apron
Away from the noise.
And there she is guided
And gains renewed strength
To find joy in her journey
And to get through her day.
Under her apron,
A woman's heart stays.
So under her apron,
A woman, she prays.

Luke 5:12–16

While Jesus was in one of the towns, a man came along who was covered with leprosy. When he saw Jesus, he fell with his face to the ground and begged him, "Lord, if you are willing, you can make me clean." Jesus reached out his hand and touched the man. "I am willing," he said. "Be clean!" And immediately the leprosy left him. Then Jesus ordered him, "Don't tell anyone, but go, show yourself to the priest and offer the sacrifices that Moses commanded for your cleansing, as a testimony to them." Yet the news about him spread all the more, so that crowds of people came to hear him and to be healed of their sicknesses. But Jesus often withdrew to lonely places and prayed.

God,

Before I begin my chores as a housewife, I need to ask You for an extra dose of courage and strength to do everything I need to do today. I place my trust You, heavenly Father, and thank You in advance for hearing and answering my prayer. In Jesus' Name, Amen.

Week Twenty Eight

Freedom

Are you hampered by your faults,
Restricted by your debt?
Let Jesus take it all from you.
Let Him leave you no regret.
Are you controlled by your past,
Held down by your sin?
Let Jesus pick it up for you
And give you peace within.
Does guilt have you burdened?
Are you shackled by your shame?
Give it all to Jesus now
And He will break the chains.
For Jesus is the way of life.
Jesus is the key.
Jesus is the truth in flesh.
The truth will set you free.

John 8:31–36 and John 14:6
To the Jews who have believed him, Jesus said, "If you
hold to my teaching, you are really my disciples. Then
you will know the truth, and the truth will set you free."
They answered him, "We are Abraham's descendants and

have never been slaves of anyone. How can you say that
we shall be set free?" Jesus replied, "I tell you the truth,
everyone who sins is a slave to sin. Now a slave has no
permanent place in the family, but a son belongs to it forever.
So if the Son sets you free, you will be free indeed.
Jesus answered, "I am the way and the truth and the
life. No one comes to the Father except through me.

Dear God,
I thank You that I live in a country where I am
free to practice my faith. I thank You for freedom
from sin through Your Son, Christ Jesus.
In Jesus' Name I pray, Amen.

Week Twenty Nine

Don't Be Finished

Sometimes we're finished.
We're finished praying.
We're finished reading.
We're finished singing.
We have to go to work,
Take care of the kids,
Answer the phone.
Sometimes we're finished trying,
Finished giving,
Finished caring,
We're finished waiting.
We feel tired,
Unappreciated,
Unheard, and alone.
But God is never finished.
He's always working for you.
So don't be finished.
Carry God in your heart
And He'll carry you when you get tired.

Galatians 6:8-10

The one who sows to please his sinful nature, from that nature will reap destruction; the one who sows to please the Spirit, from the Spirit will reap eternal life. Let us not become weary in doing good, for at the proper time we will reap a harvest if we do not give up. Therefore, as we have opportunity, let us do good to all people, especially to those who belong to the family of believers.

Dear God,

Impress upon my heart to be an encourager of my Christian brothers and sisters. In this world we all get quite enough discouragement. Do we need more in the body of believers? Thank you for giving me the gift of encouragement. Help me to use it wisely and not to grow weary in doing so.

In Jesus' Name, Amen.

Week Thirty

A Holy Friend

Thank You Holy Spirit.
Thank You Holy Friend.
Thank You for Your presence,
Residing without end.
Thank You for Your guidance
When I cannot find my way.
Thank You for Your presence
That gets me through each day.
Thank You for revealing things
I just don't understand.
Thank You for the prompting
To give a helping hand.
Thank You for the warning
When danger lies ahead.
Thank You for the ideas
That You place inside my head.
Thank You for Your prayers
When I know not what to say.
Thank You for reminding me
To be thankful every day.

Thank You for Your presence,
Abiding without end.
Thank You Holy Spirit.
Thank You Holy Friend.

John 14:25-28
"All this I have spoken while still with you. But the
Counselor, the Holy Spirit, whom the Father will send in
my name, will teach you all things and will remind you of
everything I have said to you. Peace I leave with you; my
peace I give you. I do not give to you as the world gives.
Do not let your hearts be troubled and do not be afraid.
"You heard me say, 'I am going away and I am coming
back to you.' If you loved me, you would be glad that I
am going to the Father, for the Father is greater than I.

Precious Holy Spirit,
Thank You for abiding in my heart. May everything
I say and do comes directly from You. Thank You for
making me better than I could ever be without You.
In Jesus' Name, Amen.

Week Thirty One

Praising God During Difficult Times

Thank You God.
Thank You for being here with me.
Thank You for hearing me
And for knowing what I'm feeling.
Thank You for understanding my feelings.
Thank You for prayer;
For allowing it and for hearing it.
Thank You for the opportunity.
Thank You for being a mighty God;
A God with a plan and a purpose.
Thank You for Your plan to use this difficult time
In a positive way.
Thank You for Your purpose
To give me hope and a future.
Thank You for giving me patience
As I wait for Your fulfillment.
Thank You for taking this painful time
And turning it into a time of praise.
Thank You for using this brokenness
To bring about my blessing,
And my blessing to bring glory to Your name.

Thank You;
Though life sometimes changes,
You never do.
Thank You for Your faithfulness and Your love.
God, I praise You.

1 Thessalonians 5:16–23
Be joyful always; pray continually; give thanks in all
circumstances, for this is God's will for you in Christ Jesus.
Do not put out the Spirit's fire; do not treat prophecies with
contempt. Test everything. Hold on to the good. Avoid every
kind of evil. May God himself, the God of peace, sanctify you
through and through. May your whole spirit, soul and body
be kept blameless at the coming of our Lord Jesus Christ.

Dear God,
You are Lord of my life whether everything is going
smoothly or things are not going so well. Today I
will read Your Holy Word, lift up my Bible to the sky
and declare that Your promises are true and I have
no reason to worry about anything in my life.
In Jesus' Name, Amen.

Week Thirty Two

Choices

When needing to create a plan,
A course of action to pursue,
First decide to follow Christ.
The answers they will come to you.
When dealing with a choice to make;
Which job to choose, which house to buy,
Make the choice to follow Christ.
The answers, they will come on time.
When needing to be confident
In the choices that you make,
First decide to follow Christ.
And He will lead the way.
Decisions you will have to make;
So many choices in this life.
But the most important one will be
For you to follow Jesus Christ.

Matthew 6:31–33
So do not worry, saying, 'What shall we eat?' or 'What
shall we drink?' or 'What shall we wear?' For the pagans
run after all these things, and your heavenly Father knows

that you need them. But seek first his kingdom and his righteousness, and all these things will be given to you as well.

Dear LORD,
The only thing I have to remember is that You come
first. Before I make any choices I need to seek you.
I will continue to pray and read Your Holy Word in
order to stay on the right path throughout my life.
In Jesus' Name, Amen.

Week Thirty Three

He's Already There

As you travel on life's pathway
Obstacles will arise;
A mountain, a valley,
A haunting dark sky.
As you walk towards that mountain
There's no need to fear.
God will face it with you
He's Already there.
Don't let yourself be troubled
'Bout what you do not know.
Be strong in the One
Who knows the way home.
Though the valleys may be deeper
Than what you care to bear,
Call on God to help you.
He's already there.
Don't try to see tomorrow,
Or the days that lie ahead.
God's not going to let you.
You have to trust in Him instead.

Take each step of your journey
With unwavering prayer.
There's no need to worry.
God's already there.

Exodus 14:13-18
Moses answered the people, "Do not be afraid. Stand firm
and you will see the deliverance the LORD will bring
you today. The Egyptians you see today you will never see
again. The LORD will fight for you; you need only be
still." Then the LORD said to Moses, "Why are you crying
out to me? Tell the Israelites to move on. Raise your staff
and stretch out your hand over the sea to divide the water
so that the Israelites can go through the sea on dry ground.
I will harden the hearts of the Egyptians so that they will
go in after them. And I will gain glory through Pharaoh
and all his army, through his chariots and his horsemen.
The Egyptians will know that I am the LORD when I
gain glory through Pharaoh, his chariots and horsemen."

Precious LORD,
What a comfort it is to my soul to know that You are
already in my future. I don't have to fear tomorrow because
You hold my hand and will face adversity with me.
Thank You, Lord! In Jesus' Name, Amen.

Week Thirty Four

Through the Fog

Sometimes I see
My life
Like a car on a highway.
I travel on
With the Son in front of me,
The light in my eyes.
As I move forward
I notice others coming away from the light
And I wonder why.
I continue on my way
And come upon a patch of fog.
It's hard to see.
I can't be sure of what's ahead,
But I keep going
In faith.
Those that I passed earlier,
Coming away from the light,
Must have turned back
In fear and doubt and unwillingness.
I continue on and

Make it through the fog,
The unknowing,
And I reach my destination.
My place in the Son.

2 Corinthians 4:16-18
Therefore we do not lose heart. Though outwardly we are
wasting away, yet inwardly we are being renewed day by
day. For our light and momentary troubles are achieving
for us an eternal glory that far outweighs them all. So we
fix our eyes not on what is seen, but on what is unseen. For
what is seen is temporary, but what is unseen is eternal.

Dear Shepherd,
I will trust You when I cannot see a clear road ahead of
me. Give me the faith to realize that Your will is always
best for me and may I be mindful to give You praise
throughout the journey. In Jesus' Name, Amen.

Week Thirty Five

I Can't Do a Day Without Jesus

I can't do the dishes.
Do the laundry or the shopping.
I can't do the cooking;
Not the slicing, or the chopping.
I can't do the helping,
Do what's right, or what pleases.
I'm worn out and weak.
I can't do a day without Jesus.
I can't do the calling,
The bill paying, the caring.
I can't do the teaching,
The giving, or the sharing.
I can't do this life;
Do what's right, or what's needed.
I'm unsure and uncertain.
I can't do a day without Jesus.
He gives me the strength
To push on and keep going.
He gives me the peace,
The will, and the knowing.

He gives me His love
And that is the reason
I move on in joy
And do every day with my Jesus.

Psalm 28:6-9
Praise be to the LORD, for he has heard my cry for mercy. The
LORD is my strength and my shield; my heart trusts in him,
and I am helped. My heart leaps for joy and I will give thanks to
him in song. The LORD is the strength of his people, a fortress
of salvation for his anointed one. Save your people and bless
your inheritance; be their shepherd and carry them forever.

Holy Spirit Who Dwells Within,
Just like a house that has been abandoned, my soul would
feel unloved and not treasured if I missed my daily alone
time with You. This world can be cold and unkind. You
offer love and compassion with the richness that fills my
soul so that I can in turn help others in Your name. My
soul is Your temple, Holy Spirit. Thou art welcome.
In Jesus' Name, Amen.

Week Thirty Six

I Am Said I Will

"I will heal.
I will acknowledge.
I will come again.
I will give you rest.
I will have mercy.
I will have compassion.
I will remain.
I will see you again.
I will be among you.
I will forgive.
The crown of life,
To you I will give.
I will be your Father.
You will be my son.
You will be my daughter.
Soon I will come.
I will be your God.
I will not leave you."
I am said,
"I will
Come and receive you."

John 14:1-4

"Do not let your hearts be troubled. Trust in God; trust also
in me. In my Father's house are many rooms; if it were not
so, I would have told you. I am going there to prepare a place
for you. And if I go and prepare a place for you, I will come
back and take you to be with me that you also may be where
I am. You know the way to the place where I am going."

Dear God,
There is nothing You can't do because You are everything!
Please help me to have the faith to trust You for my every need.
In Jesus' Name, Amen.

Week Thirty Seven

God's Family in Harmony

What's better than glorifying God?
Glorifying God again.
What speaks louder than a
Voice of one?
A voice of one and a friend.
Jesus said, "For where two or three have
gathered together in My name,
I am there in their midst."
Gather therefore, with your family in Christ.
How can we get big results
If we continue to live small;
If we don't join forces
In spreading the word of God,
If we don't join hearts
When to our God we pray,
If we don't join voices
In singing to Him praise?
And to join with one another
We must keep a hold of peace,
Living in acceptance,
Helping others to succeed.

Bear each other's burdens,
Build each other up,
Our voices then will harmonize
And we'll glorify our God
Again and again.

Romans 15:5-10
May the God who gives endurance and encouragement give
you a spirit of unity among yourselves as you follow Christ
Jesus, so that with one heart and mouth may glorify the God
and Father of our LORD Jesus Christ. Accept one another,
then, just as Christ accepted you, in order to bring praise
to God. For I tell you that Christ has become a servant of
the Jews on behalf of God's truth, to confirm the promises
made to the patriarchs so that the Gentiles may glorify
God for his mercy, as it is written: "Therefore I will praise
you among the Gentiles; I will sing hymns to your name."
Again, it says, "Rejoice, O Gentiles, with his people."

Dear God,
I pray that You would help me get along with my brothers
and sisters in Christ. I know that You love all of us and
want us to work together for Your glory and honor.
In Jesus' Name, Amen.

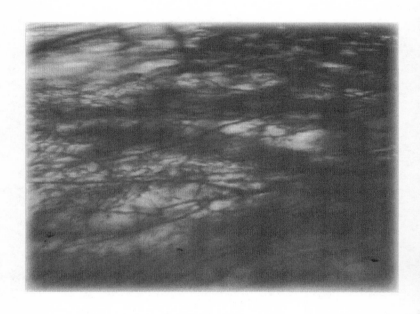

God's Shadows

Even with the shadows God creates His beauty.
Do you feel your life's a shadow;
Dark, damaged, and unnoticed?
God can still make good with you
And put things into focus.
He may just use your spirit,
Your wisdom, or your hands.
But be assured He'll use you
In the place in which you stand.
From ashes He makes beauty.
From mourning there is cheer.
He uses the weak and lowly ones
To make His message clear.
Even with the shadows
His beauty, God creates.
For He can make a blessing
From a life full of mistakes.

Isaiah 61:3-4
and provide for those who grieve in Zion—to bestow
on them a crown of beauty instead of ashes, the oil of
gladness instead of mourning, and a garment of praise

instead of a spirit of despair. They will be called oaks of righteousness, a planting of the LORD for the display of his splendor. They will rebuild the ancient ruins and restore the places long devastated; they will renew the ruined cities that have been devastated for generations.

Precious LORD,
You bless me with beauty for ashes. I make mistakes and You just keep loving me. Thank you for being so patient and not giving up on me.
In Jesus' Name, Amen.

Week Thirty Nine

He Made Me Tougher

Evil made me cry in fear.
He made my smile frown.
He made me sad, he made me mad
But he couldn't keep me down.
Nothing can keep me shackled.
My God has much more might.
He makes me bigger, He makes me better.
My God is on my right.
Evil made me doubt myself.
He brought such gloom around.
He hurt my body, he hurt my heart
But he couldn't keep me down.
God lifted me from his clutches.
He took me from his hold.
God made me calm, He made me strong
I'm free and full of hope.

Psalm 1:1-3
Blessed is the man who does not walk in the counsel of the
wicked or stand in the way of sinners or sit in the seat of
mockers. But his delight is in the law of the LORD, and on
his law he meditates day and night. He is like a tree planted

by streams of water, which yields its fruit in season and whose leaf does not whither. Whatever he does prospers.

Dear Heavenly Father,
Thank You for making me stronger and more courageous in my life than I've ever been! I can be bold and beautiful, like a tree planted by water with deep roots.
In Jesus' Name, Amen.

Week Forty

Fall in Love

When life's winds are getting strong
And your steps are unsteady,
When you think you're 'bout to fall,
Fall in love, fall in mercy.
When your foundation starts to crack,
When your world begins to shake,
When you feel that you are sinking,
Sink in love, sink in grace.
When everything looks dark
And you cannot find your way,
When you're starting to get lost,
Get lost in love. Get lost in grace.
When you feel you're being pulled,
When you're starting to get dizzy,
When you think you're 'bout to fall,
Fall in love, fall in mercy.
Fall
In the arms of Jesus.

Isaiah 40:9-10
You who bring good tidings to Zion, go up on a high
mountain. You who bring good tidings to Jerusalem, lift up

your voice with a shout, lift it up, do not be afraid; say to the towns of Judah, "Here is your God!" See, the Sovereign LORD comes with power, and his arm rules for him. See, his reward is with him, and his recompense accompanies him.

Kind Heavenly Father,
I thank you for staying close by my side. When I fall, may it always be into Your strong arms. In Jesus' Name, Amen.

Week Forty One

Pray for Your Heart

Pray for your heart
That it would be softened,
That it would be clean
From all sin and shame.
Pray for your heart
That it would be focused
Only on Jesus
And His precious name.
Pray for your heart
That it would be patient,
That it would show kindness
To those who're in need.
Pray for your heart
That it'd reflect Jesus
With every breath,
With every beat.

Colossians 3:7-10
You used to walk in these ways, in the life you once lived.
But now you must rid yourselves of all such things as these:
anger, rage, malice, slander, and filthy language from your
lips. Do not lie to each other, since you have taken off your

old self with its practices and have put on the new self, which is being renewed in knowledge in the image of its Creator.

Dear God,
I pray You would give me a soft heart, a clean heart focused only on Jesus and His precious Name. I pray that You would help me to bless someone else even if I am going through my own storm. Please give me patience and kindness when I'm dealing with others.
In Jesus' Name, Amen.

Week Forty Two

Finding Home

Once abandoned, all alone
I wandered through my life.
I felt so lonely and unwanted.
So many times I cried.
I had no friends or family.
No love from anyone.
It was hard to keep on going.
I felt nothing could be done.
Then once when I was roaming,
I felt that I was led
To a place of warmth and light
And there my heart was fed.
I nestled next to Jesus.
He let me rest with Him.
He carried things I couldn't.
He gave me His right hand.
With Jesus I found family.
My true forever home.
I'll never be rejected.
I'll never be alone.

I say this 'cause I hope to
Encourage those who're lost
To curl up next to Jesus.
He'll love you at all costs.

Psalm 34:14-22
Turn from evil and do good; seek peace and pursue it.
The eyes of the LORD are on the righteous and his ears
are attentive to their cry; the face of the LORD is against
those who do evil, to cut off the memory of them from the
earth. The righteous cry out, and the LORD hears them;
he delivers them from their troubles. The LORD is close to
the brokenhearted and saves those who are crushed in spirit.
A righteous man may have many troubles, but the LORD
delivers him from them all; he protects all his bones, not one
of them will be broken. Evil will slay the wicked; the foes of
the righteous will be condemned. The LORD redeems his
servants; no one will be condemned who take refuge in him.

Abba Father,
Thank You for letting me nestle next to You when
I feel lost and alone. You will never leave me or
forsake me. You are my forever family.
In Jesus' Name, Amen.

Week Forty Three

A Sip, A prayer, A Peace

A spot of tea.
A comfy chair.
A light and dainty treat.
Take a sip.
Say a prayer
And feel His gift of peace.
Sipping slowly.
A book in hand.
A loved pet at your feet.
Praising God
For all He's planned.
His best is yet to be.
Breath the freshness
In the air
And feel His mighty hand,
Sip your tea,
Say a prayer,
And feel His peace again.

Colossians 3:15-17
Let the peace of Christ rule in your hearts, since as
members of one body you were called to peace. And be

thankful. Let the word of Christ dwell in you richly as you teach and admonish one another with all wisdom, and as you sing psalms, hymns, and spiritual songs with gratitude in your hearts to God. And whatever you do, whether in word or deed, do it all in the name of the Lord Jesus, giving thanks to God the Father through him.

God of Peace,
I thank You for calming my mind and spirit with a simple thing like a cup of tea and a book. So often we seek peace in the wrong places when we should be seeking You. Your way of escape from stress is always best.
In Jesus' Name, Amen.

Week Forty Four

How to Sleep Through a Storm

Is your life in the midst of a storm today?
Do you feel things are out of control?
The Bible tells us to imitate Jesus.
Jesus, He slept through a storm.
He wasn't worried or afraid
He had complete control of it.
You may not be in full control
But you can trust the One who is.
Trust in the One who blows the wind,
The One who created the sea.
Rely on Him who calms the waters.
Imitate Jesus and believe.
He will bring you through this trial.
Do not worry, do not fret.
Trust in Jesus to calm the storm.
This faith will help you rest.

Mark 4:35–40

That day when evening came, he said to his disciples, "Let us
go over to the other side." Leaving the crowd behind, they took
him along, just as he was, in the boat. There were also other
boats with him. A furious squall came up, and the waves broke

over the boat, so that it was nearly swamped. Jesus was in the stern, sleeping on a cushion. The disciples woke him and said to him, "Teacher, don't you care if we drown?" He got up, rebuked the wind and said to the waves, "Quiet! Be still!" Then the wind died down and it was completely calm. He said to his disciples, "Why are you so afraid? Do you still have no faith?"

Father of Peace,
Just as You spoke peace unto the literal storm, speak peace unto the storm in my life right now. Please grant me courage and strength to face these things head on with boldness and confidence that only You can provide.
In Jesus' Name, Amen.

Week Forty Five

A God of Always

We sometimes read our Bible.
God always has a message.
We sometimes pray before meals.
God always provides.
We sometimes go to church.
God is always there.
We sometimes ask for guidance.
God always knows the way.
We sometimes help a neighbor.
God always helps us.
We sometimes forgive a wrong.
God is always willing to forgive us.
We sometimes spend time in prayer.
God always takes time to answer.
We sometimes look past someone's flaws.
God sees all of ours and always looks past them.
We sometimes give God Glory.
God always deserves it.
We sometimes sing songs of praise.
God always sings over us.
We're sometimes a people of sometimes.
But God is always a God of always.

Hebrews 10:22-23
let us draw near to God with a sincere heart in full
assurance of faith, having our hearts sprinkled to cleanse
us from a guilty conscience and having our bodies
washed with pure water. Let us hold unswervingly to
the hope we profess, for he who promised is faithful.

Precious Lord,
My devotion to You can seem almost slipshod
compared to Your consistent, constant love and
care for me. You are Lord of my life and I want
nothing more than Your perfect will in my life.
In Jesus' Name, Amen.

Week Forty Six

God's Feet

God's feet are next to your feet.
His hands are near your hands.
Whether you walk the beach
Or busy streets
God is where you stand.
God's feet are next to your feet.
His heart is near your heart.
If you're with a friend
Or alone again
God is with you from the start.
God's feet are next to your feet.
He feels whatever you feel;
A painful tease,
A gentle squeeze.
His presence always real.
God's feet are next to your feet.
His ear is near your voice.
He hears your words.
He hears your cries.
He hears your lips rejoice.

God's feet are next to your feet
And never will he leave.
He loved you then.
He loves you now.
He'll love you eternally.

Psalm 139:7–12
Where can I go from your Spirit? Where can I flee from your
presence? If I go up to the heavens, you are there; if I make
my bed in the depths, you are there. If I rise on the wings of
the dawn, if I settle on the far side of the sea, even there your
hand will guide me, your right hand will hold me fast. If I say,
"Surely the darkness will hide me and the light become night
around me," even the darkness will not be dark to you; the
night will shine like the day, for darkness is as light to you.

Dear God,
It means so much to me that You are right by my
side as I live my life. There is nothing to fear because
You love me and listen to me when I pray.
In Jesus' Name, Amen.

Week Forty Seven

Pressed and Praising

Do you ever feel stretched
Like a tightened rubber band?
Do you ever feel so pressed
You think you cannot stand?
Do you ever feel abandoned
Left to do it all by yourself?
Do you ever feel so lost
You can't find your own way out?
Be encouraged!
God's there to carry your burdens
And He knows the trusted way.
God will replace your energy
And He can reshape your days.
You are not abandoned.
You're never left alone.
God is always with you
Even from the throne.
He will see you through this
So Jesus will be seen,
And glory it'd be given
To Christ, our God and King.
Praise Him!

Psalm 94:16–19

Who will rise up for me against the wicked? Who will
take a stand for me against evildoers? Unless the LORD
have given me help, I would soon have dwelt in the
silence of death. When I said, "My foot is slipping," your
love, O LORD, supported me. When anxiety was great
within me, your consolation brought joy to my soul.

Lord of All,

Your consolation during times of stress and trouble is
priceless. The comfort You speak to my soul means so
much to me. I know nothing can harm me because You
protect me. No matter how much pressure I feel today,
I will rejoice in You and Your precious Holy Word.
In Jesus' Name, Amen.

Meet Him in Your Prayers

Are you looking for direction,
Someone to be your guide?
Meet God in your prayers tonight.
He's always by your side.
Does happiness seem impossible?
You think you cannot cope.
Meet God in your prayers tonight.
He will give you hope.
Are you looking for life's answers?
Are you looking for some peace?
Meet God in your prayers tonight.
He will meet your needs.
Are you looking for a loving friend,
Someone to see you through?
Meet God in your prayers tonight.
He's always there for you.
Do you need someone to hold your hand
Before you come apart?
Meet God in your prayers tonight.
He will hug your heart.
He's waiting.

Isaiah 43:1-3

But now, this is what the LORD says--he who created you, O Jacob, he who formed you, O Israel: "Fear not, for I have redeemed you; I have summoned you by name; you are mine. When you pass through the waters, I will be with you; and when you pass through the rivers, they will not sweep over you. When you walk through the fire, you will not be burned; the flames will not set you ablaze. For I am the LORD, your God, the Holy One of Israel, your Savior;

Father,

Today I pray for my friends and family, and myself. For those who are experiencing grief, loss, or other pain whether it be physical or emotional. I pray You would give us comfort, peace of mind, and encouragement of heart. Please put Your arms around us letting us know it will be ok. Thank You for loving us and protecting us through the night.

In Jesus' Name, Amen.

Photo by Stephanie Guier L Photography

Week Forty Nine

Finding Joy in the Journey

Today I'll step forward,
Accept all the struggles,
Bear all the burdens and pain,
Fight through the obstacles,
Stand firm in the battles,
To bring all glory to His name.
There's no need in Heaven
To bring God the glory.
His glory it will be known.
I need to do that
Here in this lifetime
Before God carries me home,
To love Him, to serve Him,
To lead others to Him,
That is what gives my life worth.
I'll find joy in the journey
By bringing God glory
In the time I have left on this earth.

Psalm 71:14–18
But as for me, I will always have hope; I will praise you
more and more. My mouth will tell of your righteousness; of

your salvation all day long, thought I know not its measure. I will come and proclaim your mighty acts, O Sovereign LORD; I will proclaim your righteousness, yours alone. Since my youth, O God, you have taught me, and to this day I declare your marvelous deeds. Even when I am old and gray, do not forsake me, O God, till I declare your power to the next generation, your might to all who are to come.

Lord of Joy,
May I be filled with Your unmistakable joy and
ready to share it with everyone I meet today!
In Jesus' Name, Amen.

Week Fifty

All the Time

Love God with all your heart,
With all your strength,
With all your soul, and
With all your mind.
Love God when you're playing,
When you're running,
When you're dancing,
Love Him when you're laughing.
Love Him when you're resting.
When you're singing,
When you're reading,
Love Him when it's quiet.
Love Him with your money,
With your talents,
With your service,
Love Him when you're working.
Love Him with your tears,
When you're aching,
When you're crying,
Love Him with your burdens.

Love Him with all your time,
With all you have,
With all you are,
Wherever you go.
Love God all the time.

Luke 10:25-28

On one occasion an expert in the law stood up to test Jesus. "Teacher," he asked, "what must I do to inherit eternal life?" "What is written in the law?" he replied. "How do you read it?" He answered: "'Love the Lord your God with all your heart and with all your soul and with all your strength and with all your mind', and 'Love your neighbor as yourself.'" "You have answered correctly," Jesus replied. "Do this and you will live."

Dear God,

Help me to love You always. Whatever I'm doing or wherever I'm going, I always want to love You with everything in me.
In Jesus' Name, Amen.

Week Fifty One

This Thing Called Life

I couldn't do this without You Lord
I wouldn't want to try.
The dishes, the laundry,
This thing called life.
I couldn't do this without You.
I wouldn't know where to start.
The stress, the tension,
The pain in my heart.
I couldn't do this without You.
This thing called life
The struggles, the hardships,
The sadness, and strife.
I couldn't do this without You.
I'm not able to get by.
But Your grace and Your mercy,
They carry me high.
Thanks for the reason,
The will, and the might,
To keep on doing
This thing called life.

Psalm 118:1-7

Give thanks to the LORD, for he is good; his love endures forever. Let Israel say: "His love endures forever." Let the house of Aaron say: "His love endures forever." Let those who fear the LORD say: "His love endures forever." In my anguish I cried to the LORD, and he answered by setting me free. The LORD is with me; I will not be afraid. What can man do to me? The LORD is with me; he is my helper.

Father God,

It's not always easy to get up every morning and face the day. Thank You so much for giving me the courage to live another day. You are my source of strength.

In Jesus' Name, Amen.

Week Fifty Two

Stumble and Fall

You can stumble and fall
By the steps that you take.
Make a mess of it all
With the choices you make.
But God never leaves you.
His love stays the same.
He watches and sees you.
Just call on His name.
He's not afraid of messes.
He can fix all mistakes.
He makes good of bad choices.
He's got all that it takes.
So put the past behind you
Right where it belongs.
Call on God to help you.
He will make you strong.
You can stumble and fall
By the choices you make.
But you can rise and fly high
By the hand that you take.

Ephesians 1:3-8

Praise be to the God and Father of our Lord Jesus Christ, who has blessed us in the heavenly realms with every spiritual blessing in Christ. For he chose us in him before the creation of the world to be holy and blameless in his sight. In love he predestined us to be adopted as his sons through Jesus Christ, in accordance with his pleasure and will -- to the praise of his glorious grace, which he has freely given us in the One he loves. In him we have redemption through his blood, the forgiveness of sins, in accordance with the riches of God's grace that he lavished on us with all wisdom and understanding.

Father of Mercy,
I claim the blood of your Son, Christ Jesus, covers my sins and transgressions. I thank You for this miracle and for the promise of Heaven when this life is over.
In Jesus' Name, Amen.

Something special written by both Linda and Lucinda

<u>God Whispers in the Wind</u>

The wind is cold, may chill your bones.
It is indeed quite blustery today.
But if you're quiet, between your shivers
You'll hear what the Lord has to say. "When
life seems cold I'll give you warmth
And whisper sweet peace to your soul.
I'll whisper words to guide and keep you
Words of wisdom to make you whole.
No need to ever feel alone
Throughout your life I will abide.
Through sun and rain, through winter's cold
I will always be by your side."
So remember to listen in the wind
Regardless of the time of year.
God will whisper to your heart
His peace will replace all your fear.

Topical Index

Encouraging words on...

Challenges
Choices — Week 32
Don't be Finished — Week 29
Fall in Love — Week 40
God's Feet — Week 46
God's Plans — Week 1
He Sees Us Through — Week 12
How to Sleep Through a Storm — Week 44
I Can't Do a Day Without Jesus — Week 35
Meet Him in Your Prayers — Week 48
Pick Up a Shovel — Week 21
Prayer by Prayer — Week 29
Pressed and Praising — Week 47
The Donkey — Week 8
This Thing Called Life — Week 51
Too Busy — Week 7
Troubles? — Week 4
Eternal Life
A God of Always — Week 45
Do-Overs — Week 23
Freedom — Week 28

He Died for Me   Week 11

He Sees Us Through   Week 12

I Am Said I Will   Week 36

I'm God's Somebody   Week 18

Faith

Fall in Love   Week 40

God's Plans   Week 1

He's Already There   Week 33

He Sees Us Through   Week 12

How to Sleep Through a Storm   Week 44

Pressed and Praising   Week 47

Through the Fog   Week 34

Too Busy   Week 7

You're Still on Your Feet   Week 14

Feelings of Guilt

Do-Overs   Week 23

Freedom   Week 28

God's Shadows   Week 38

Stumble and Fall   Week 52

The Baggage Carrier   Week 5

God's Love for You

A God of Always   Week 45

Finding Home   Week 42

I Am Said I Will   Week 36

Live Like You're Loved   Week 26

Message from the Sun   Week 3

Not Enough Soup   Week 15

When You Just Want to Go to Sleep   Week 19

Who Is The Holy Spirit?   Week 6

God's Mercy

Finding Home   Week 42

Freedom   Week 28

Stumble and Fall   Week 52

God's Presence

A God of Always   Week 45

God's Feet   Week 46

He's Already There   Week 33

His Right Arm   Week 2

A Holy Friend   Week 30

I Am Said I Will   Week 36

I Can't Do a Day Without Jesus   Week 35

Meet Him in Your Prayers   Week 48

Message from the Sun   Week 3

Who Is The Holy Spirit?   Week 6

Hope

God's Plans   Week 1

He Sees Us Through   Week 12

Message from the Sun   Week 3

You're Still on Your Feet   Week 14

Loving God

All the Time   Week 50

God's Family in Harmony   Week 37

Just to Praise Him   Week 20

Live Like You're Loved   Week 26

Seek Him   Week 22

Peace

Fall in Love   Week 40

Finding Home   Week 42

When You Just Want to Go to Sleep   Week 19
Prayer
A Sip, A Prayer, A Peace   Week 43
Meet Him in Your Prayers   Week 48
Praising God in Difficult Times   Week 31
Prayer by Prayer   Week 9
Pray for Your Heart   Week 41
Pressed and Praising   Week 47
Under Her Apron   Week 27
Serving God
Don't be Finished   Week 29
Finding Joy in the Journey   Week 49
God's Family in Harmony   Week 37
Invisible Me   Week 10
Live Like You're Loved   Week 26
Sycamore Trees   Week 16
The Cross of Christ in Your Life   Week 13
Use Your Gifts   Week 24
Your Pain Their Blessing   Week 17
Your Own Self Worth
Freedom   Week 28
God's Shadows   Week 38
God the Knitter   Week 25
He Died for Me   Week 11
He Made Me Tougher   Week 39
I'm God's Somebody   Week 18

Scripture Index

Exodus 14:13–18	Week 33
Deuteronomy 31:6–8	Week 3
1 Chronicles 16:8–13.	Week 9
Psalm 1:1–3	Week 39
Psalm 4:5–8	Week 19
Psalm 28:6–9	Week 35
Psalm 34:14–22	Week 42
Psalm 71:14–18	Week 49
Psalm 71:19–22	Week 12
Psalm 89:13–15	Week 2
Psalm 94:16–19	Week 47
Psalm 103:8–14	Week 23
Psalm 105:1–5	Week 22
Psalm 118:1–7	Week 52
Psalm 121	Week 14
Psalm 138:1–4	Week 20
Psalm 138:4–8	Week 18
Psalm 139:7–12	Week 46
Psalm 139:13–18	Week 25
Psalm 145:13–19	Week 5
Psalm 145:18–21	Week 7
Isaiah 26:3–8	Week 4
Isaiah 40:9–10	Week 40

Isaiah 43:1-3	Week 48
Isaiah 61:3-4	Week 38
Jeremiah 29:10-13	Week 1
Matthew 6:31-33	Week 32
Mark 4:35-40	Week 45
Luke 5:12-16	Week 27
Luke 10:25-28	Week 50
Luke 19:1-6	Week 16
John 8:31-36 and John 14:6	Week 28
John 14:1-4	Week 36
John 14:15-17	Week 6
John 14:25-28	Week 30
Romans 15:5-10	Week 37
1 Corinthians 10:1-6	Week 17
1 Corinthians 12:4-11	Week 24
2 Corinthians 4:16-18	Week 34
Galatians 6:8-10	Week 29
Ephesians 1:3-8	Week 51
Ephesians 2:8-10	Week 15
Ephesians 4:1-3	Week 13
Colossians 3:7-10	Week 41
Colossians 3:15-17	Week 43
1 Thessalonians 5:16-23	Week 31
2 Thessalonians 1:11-12	Week 21
Hebrews 6:10-12	Week 10
Hebrews 10:22-23	Week 45
1 John 2:1-2	Week 11
1 John 3:18 and 23-24	Week 26
1 John 5:3-5	Week 8

Christian Website Links

Linda Palmer author of prayers included in this book also has several sites where she offers words of encouragement and support with a little humor.
Hearthungerblog.wordpress.com/
w ww.facebook.com/poetryformysavior/timeline
w ww.facebook.com/bless.God.today.America
americablessgodtoday.webs.com/

Stephanie Guier Lutz ---Photo with Week 49
Thank you God because through my camera lens I can appreciate better what You have created. A page dedicated to share my photography.
www.facebook.com/StephanieGuierLPhotography

Under His Wings is a bestselling devotional collection of real-life bird encounters enjoyed by author, Joy DeKok. You don't have to be a birdwatcher to enjoy the stories or the life-changing truths in this delightful book.
www.amazon.com/Under-His-Wings-Joy-DeKok-ebook/dp/B00D6OMLRM/ref=sr_1_2?ie=UTF8&qid=1404759691&sr=8-2&keywords=joy+dekok

TM Brown - Struggles of the Women Folk. This is the story of Georgie. She is a young black girl growing up in the 1940s in a small, rural town in Virginia. Her life is hard and she dreams of better life. She loses friends, family, and the love of her life under circumstances that are difficult to accept. And still, she remains strong.
www.amazon.com/Struggles-Women-Folk-T-Brown-ebook/dp/B00KAOYBWY/ref=la_B00BTFCLAW_sp-atf_title_1_2?s=books&ie=UTF8&qid=1405549821&sr=1-2

New Testament Life
Mission To encourage and inspire you to live the New Testament Life by stimulating your senses such as sight, hearing, smell, and touch with Christian products that surround and enrich your life.
Company Overview
Your Soul Provider for all your Christian Resource Needs For any Season of your Life
w ww.newtestamentlife.com

Life is a Garden Party, Vol. II by Judy Janowski.
A gardening observation with a spiritual application in rhyme.
bookstore.westbowpress.come/Products/SKU-000735604/Life-Is-a-Garden-Party-Volume-II.aspx
Blog: lifeisagardenparty.blogspot.com

Cyndi's Light Work Designs
Christian gifts, inspirational designs, banners, bookmarks, note and greeting cards, and personalized keepsakes.
We color your canvas with light and purpose.
w ww.cyndisdesignz.com/

Made in the USA
Middletown, DE
31 August 2018